Monologue of Fire

Monologue of Fire

Samuel Ugbechie

Many Voices Project Winner #144

©2022 by Samuel Ugbechie
First Edition
Library of Congress Control Number: 2021937316
ISBN: 978-0-89823-405-3

New Rivers Press is a nonprofit literary press associated with Minnesota State University Moorhead.

Cover design by Brianna Jensen
Interior design by Nayt Rundquist
Author photo by Samuel Ugbechie
The publication of *Monologue of Fire* is made possible by the generous support of Minnesota State University Moorhead, the Dawson Family Endowment, and other contributors to New Rivers Press.

NRP Staff: Nayt Rundquist, Managing Editor; Kevin Carollo, Editor; Travis Dolence, Director; Trista Conzemius, Art Director
Interns: Katie Betz, Jaeda Engberg, Alex Ferguson, Shaina Garman, Andrew Reed, Sam Schroeder

Monologue of Fire book team: Alex Ferguson, Shaina Garman, Geneva Nodland, Azim Usmanov, Grace Vetrone

 Printed in the USA on acid-free, archival-grade paper.

Monologue of Fire is distributed nationally by Small Press Distribution.

 New Rivers Press
c/o MSUM
1104 7th Ave S
Moorhead, MN 56563
www.newriverspress.com

Contents

I

II

III

IV

I

Scars of utterance

Unlike ink, blood doesn't pour,
                              it pleads. So mom, in this cohort
of the dark, in this night dipped into warmth, I cannot write you in ocher,
the color
of longing, the blood that plaits
                              the cadence of dreaming, the honey
that pinches our sleeping cells. I cannot mail you my sigh

in palms of singing if I still sleep
                              soul-bare with a necklet of scars
alighting from my dream like a drizzle, if, tonight, a plea
still flames my eyes, if, tonight,
                              the dark that spills
the night still simmers in me. There's an utterance

of dawn on the laundry
                              of my breath, and through the feverish wind
-falls between us, a stone falls like the droppings of a wren,
splays like what stays when grief
                              is grilled by its own
song. Sure, there are sounds that will never find their tongues,

breaths that will never find
                              their lungs, nails that will never find
their toes. But here's your womb, night. Find her. Hurl me
with a thousand rays rising
                              like a cushion in my ribs,
and let me break like a lung-greased sigh, let me crack

like a swollen dirge, let me be
                        where I was when I could be nothing
else but a babble, but a ballot of flavors, a tongue-sweet
weeping, a bone-savory bleeding.
                        Let me be where I was
when the world was just your word, and all I could clench

was your syntax of lull
                        -abies, the avalanche of your silences drummed
between us like deftness, like the clime of brokenness in rain, the timber
of a soul on top of its soil. Let me be
                        you again shrunk
and plucked, tucked into the tincture that doesn't tar

a soul, dipped into the umber never under
                        what floats, never under the tide
that neither died nor dried, nor sighed into silence. Fling
your body into this wind dressed
                        like a second shot,
like a second snipe at harmony, at ashes and song,

at the burr of beauty and bleeding and love.

Two bleeding sidewalls of dark

The night is tinged like the loam on the traffic lanes
of a vein. The night is a tongue-rail, a bulletin of skins

tasting like the timber that spits off the fiber
of a moose. The night is you and I alike, two lights

too shy to flame, dimming out of their bones through
an organelle of cuddling. The night wants you the way

a habit wants its human, the way this turbulence
is a belching soul, the way belonging is the flag

of a tongue greased by an ocean that gazes at a city
in ruins. Tonight, a new night will come, and rail us

into dawn, and we shall carry the night before—
veiled like the innards of a vow—down to the city

center, weeping like a throne plucked from a whisker
with prickles as its crown. We shall drip liquid ash,

a fluid darkness, the fluent soot of two souls alloyed
into tongue. We shall taste the bassinet of our bones

lost inside a torn, taut tunnel. We shall be ovaries
ripened in sunlight, organs pushing out of leaking paths,

irises spreading on a road on diet. We shall sing
like murmur and memory, like a broken arm beneath

a mound of kisses. We shall be you and I astray
like the anther of a wish, like the droppings of rain

tender like the climate of a dialogue salted in a dirge
of rays, as smooth as the topology of a glance bent

between the tides of two colliding songs. We shall stretch
our legs from dawn to noon, and our hungers

will unwrap like kindness into another night, into another
tale, say fossils for the frail, dactyls for the day,

say songs don't burn except the tongue is a sea-strong
plastic of spittle and special, say me and you a sleeve

as slim as virtue, a love as songs pinned by the beak
of a dove, say a bird is our fellowship on the radius of fire,

on the marrow biking out of the morrow like an ache
biking out of a bone.

Thirst is home-made

Back home, a storm hissed
                    in our bellies, and walked into us
like a chuckle. The nectars of breath we mounted, the hunger-ripped
ballads that poured out on us like murmurs,
                              turned into the only surviving cliff
of our once-crushed conversation. Mother,

I'm a tamarind buried
                  on your belly like a pore. I've gone
nowhere farther than the flourish on your navel. I've found you by escaping:
the warring paths that tar
                          the staccatos on my tongue, the cities
that weep a cleft off my semi-detached soul. Still,

I call you tonight if only your voice
                          would tide and hide me again
in this rehearsal of solitude tatted on my back like a rash, in which I scratch
your upholstered body, which ages
                              like a vase, which bleeds like an oil
-can of regrets, from which I tip and sip daily, knowing,

in the song trussed in this melon
                          of dissonance, distance, like hunger
or thirst, never shrinks. The more we machine this moment, I find me leaf-
ing
a petal, flowering a candle
                        -wick out of my breath. And rain washes
my skin into a yolk. The orchids of my lungs cry

over their woven peels,
$\qquad$ and I spill a million rinds of sorry,
and rust in their moon-blank checks, from where you yell *no* again,
longing for the body of the voice,
$\qquad$ and not the voice of the body.
Wanting the ocean and not its lining of eddies

and ebbs. And I wish I could mail
$\qquad$ the demo of my soul and sigh
to you, the sculpture of my silence in toes of fire, all garmented
like the diapered lullabies
$\qquad$ of the ruptured currencies
we shared back home, to which I gift

this silence, to which I bury
$\qquad$ this song in the countless ant
-hills that separate us, each the mound of melody or misery, each the grape
-fruit that growls, each blending into
$\qquad$ the tilt of the night,
all sore and sown, all coalescing into the story that belches

in our veins like a cork
$\qquad$ -screw tightening us, like an anthem sewn
into harmony, stitched into a chorus as cracked as a loss.

Rapprochement

The room is an infantry
                    of secrets, replete with decade
-old whispers, where I sang like a word unsaid in the console
of your silence. Tonight, the room
                              is a swivel chair, the stutter
of toys, the mattress with a buried breath. At times,

the room was me. No key
                    keen enough could pierce
me into rain. The room, today, is you and I fused and faded into fire.
I'm hidden, tonight, like a song
                        plucked off a finger,
like the woman in *The Old Guitarist*, unseen

until she's seen, all those infrared
                              waves intoned like infinite
lens, tiding what ebbs, howling what hushes, pulling the string that grazes
on the murmurs peppered in the fissure
                              of a soul. Let's talk,
tonight. Let's clang and cleave again. Let's walk

into our windows like the weather
                        that squirms within a phrase,
or a page. Like the touch that greases a memory until it leaks. You and I,
two birds untethered, a distance-broken,
                              the years splashed against our fat,
frozen wounds. I'll only heal, I guess, by unsealing

the flannel of my scar. I'll only heal
                              if nothing but your cleft
obscures me, until the hours that quake in this room come apart
like solitude, and all our regrets
                              regress into ash, and lash,
even now, like longing juiced in a gourd,

like a yearning awakened in the stiffened
                              strands of our vehicular
veins, where, tonight, we journey by crying and creaking like the past,
by arriving here again, in this room
                              of ache and age, in this room
of a seism fleeing the fuselage of our stomach-fitted souls.

All the lines that do not lead me home

I wish I could sing
　　　　　　on every sigh I flew on to the present. I wish
the bruise on my rib wasn't as free as a hand
-sewn flame. Let the song wrung

out of a bowl drag me
　　　　　　through a thigh of departure. Let me
through the room found in the fist of a fruit, a home as rich
as silence, wild as a moon

-deep mutter, as taut
　　　　　　as the crack that spills a country into our sleep.
Fruit-fingered memory, fruit-thick chin, rib
and femur me into flutes. I'm painting, tonight,

a scar of nostalgia.
　　　　　　So bear with me for a while. The yard, though—
the rain-torn colony of ants, the pasture painted softly
in a clench—is your oblong face on my oolong

face tonight. Tell me, mom,
　　　　　　isn't the stutter of the sea our breaths
and deaths going at it? Isn't a country a bone
-cracked cuticle, sans seeds, sans

skin, sans silence? *No,*
　　　　　　you say—a factory of frowns on your glance,
behind which your tongue flicks and plucks a finger
of love off your soul. I don't want to grow

old until I've cried the umpteenth
                              time as a child in your arms forever.
What we have is as habitable as water, where a ghost
could swim out of a tide, where a body

could body, could skin,
                              could tissue and issue out of laughter. Tonight,
in the room, I look at your photo the way a mile looks at distance,
the way a ray looks at the sun, the way

an itch looks at its scratch.
                              Thirst is your koine on my tongue, pronouncing
every ache as *home*, as *touch*, as *blood*. The moon blurs
and blurs until your eye is the only stucco

on the stadia of the dark,
                              thickening like the pulse on which a breath kittens
it juice afresh. But every taste owns a tongue. Every touch hides
a scar in its purse. Every death seals a breath

in its bone. In the room,
                              my soul—the pale-olive, the kiss-ripped, the slack
-jawed loin of nectar—sneezes back into my rib
from an abattoir of longing.

And bleeding is the only route
                              I know to needing, to kneading a thirst
and hanging it like devotion on my lungs, to knotting
a question like copper strings in my throat,

to *hatchling* and *calf*
                              -*ling*, to *duckling* and *chickling* and *gosling* alone.
I'm *fingerling* at home, mom, from the owlet in the outlet
bled by your absence, in which I whelp and help

12

myself to songs,
            to sea, and to sigh, and to a silence that knifes out
a flush of beauty off the empire of your warmth.

Familial currencies

At dawn, I hug my mother close as though
I were hammering a silence through her soul.
                              Near the battery of her belly
I charge the veins that buoy memories,
my body is an unspooled finger, tinkering into flowers.

We sit at the corridor as though
the world has paused its dance, and
                              count three hundred corpses
in our ash-striped eyes. Today,
I scratch the quake that performs a mother's touch

like a plum. I hold a cantaloupe of silence
and bleed it till it howls, honeying the fossil
                              my mother fetches
out of waiting. To leave or not to leave?
To strum a distance with my tongue or to juice a distance

into one? I don't want to cry if my soul gurgles
like my only heart-beat steam. I don't want
                              to leave if leaving
is my bone dashed into a distant womb.
The morning digests the dark, and an apron of light breaks

out of the bluntest path through my mother's
eyes. I cannot look her in the eyes and not
                              become the baby
painted crisply in her womb. We walk down
the loyal paths, fork a solitude till it unseals a sea

above the salt-level of the thirst that slaps
us into love. Bottle-brown route, moss
                                        -grown path, what foot
-fall have I felled sourly on the torso
of my past? Fin-burred bodies, why doesn't doubt dim

and drown me when its dives into me like an augury?
Why isn't my mind awake like the ache
                                        that pins me down
to a pulse? I know the itch that splits
a scratch. I know shared blood, and my hair,

and its fence barbed by a flush of maternal
fragrance. I know my skin. I know a thing or two
                                        about the taste tonguing
a brooklet in you. And I know the angle
we aim to breathe, or yield, or the part of the lung

that's a path never tarred. Here's my heart.
Wring out its last oil. Taste and glue
                                        your tongue to fire. Misfire
your soul into a mist that undresses
into melody. Take me by the hand, mom,

until when I leave I won't, when I go I don't.
Until rain falls like inflection on our walk,
                                        and the sleep we did
not sleep slips out of us like a possum,
shadows us like the night that's neither right nor wrong,

dusk nor dawn, a grief sandwiched between your sigh
and yawn, a time stretching like what love
                                        birdlimes into us,
from trying, and trying, and trying painfully again.

Swallowed by memories

Because my body is a parcel of sighs.
Because every window is an alphabet

slung from a wind that tattles
to a wounded gull. Because warren.

Because oak and frost labor hard
into the staircase of the woods.

Because my skin is the shroud
of my skeleton. Because my bone

is a scroll on which my blood is a tale.
Because country. Because vine

-gar is the chorus of the throat,
slithering out of the hole wrapped

in the towel of a chest-built tunnel.
Because I love you and still shrink.

Because my mouth is a message
of ciders, a pink massage of sesames.

Because you will go again, your stare
the creek of a crane, the beast

of a ballad leaping off your tongue
like a secret in a possum's fist.

Because paw on the soul is the thaw
-ing of war, is ice singing with broken

teeth, is rain reversed, grinding the sky
into ash. Because memories. Because

my bones are feasting on the rail
of a toe. Because melody is born

not made. Because, here in the salsa
of the sun, you will widen like the foot

-work of a ray, the tension written
in the rain, the lexicon of water buried

in the burrow of a mind swallowed
by its memories.

Songs in an urn

To taste the chapel of a kiss, to touch
the sesame of dark, how the spinach

of the night bends for silence, how the lineage
of a tongue tips the cider of its own skin.

To shrink inside the sleeve of longing,
to know not all songs belong to their own virtues.

Tonight, we are two bodies in a vase, written
in salt and olive. Still, silence fragments

us, as though a thousand ribs of vowels
have broken out of us, as if the kindness

of our lips is now a sepulture of bones.
To become belonging we mesh into the gauze

that bleeds on the forepart of a dream,
and, in that season pinching the navel

of our sleep, I go where nightmares pile
themselves, and return with the moon

cata-cornered like question marks on my skin.
I'm the question with a beard and a bone,

and you alone know how my knuckles
thrum, how they feast on the fires that fist

them, how they become the music on the rear
of a bee gum, how they become a song slung

into the lungs of a hive, and, shriveled
like the mood of a nerve tonight, I ache

to know you the way a cork knows its gourd,
the way strife cuts without its knife, the way

a body belches its weapon within, knowing
every thirst is a sofa on the soul, crying

for a breathing peel, a sniffing rind, a night
afraid of its own dark, a silence like yours,

terraced with a bone, and a skin, and a breath
that bulges thickly out of singing.

My soul is a fortuity of songs

My body, tonight, is a monologue of fire,
those memories that bite
                            my sleep like music
on the fulcrum
of the soul, ashes that sift like laurels

made of umber on the loneliest tongues
of the night. There is a top
                            -ology of solitude
on my veins tonight,
as if, in an instant, I was lowered down

like songs on a bulletin of bones, as if, in an instant,
a molecule of my mother's
                            glance spilled like firm
-aments on my skin,
as if, in an instant, the distance between here

and home is an island washing off my bones
through a contagion of calm.
                    I know just one country,
my mother,
whose thought is a ballot on my brain, whose syntax

is the lexicon of grit that tours me, whose voice
is a console of the vow
                    -els, singing back to me,
every night,
from the lullabies greasing the fore of my child

-hood, from what pours from *dark* to *dear*, from what falls
from *dream* to *dazzle*.
                              There's a night on every child,
a shroud that creaks
open as though every soul were an enclosure

of songs, as though to grow is to leaven a memory,
as though motherhood
                              is a thick soliloquy
of flowers,
which no mile could rust, which, drizzling

down tonight, becomes the cartridge of a silence
floating and spilling,
                              becoming a virtue
unleashed like flying
in an avalanche of soft, enatic hums.

Breakfast is a thousand flavors

In Cassatt's *Breakfast in Bed*, you and I thirst again,
    hungry, as if eternity had leaked out of our stomachs,

as if the cup could swill us down for the rest of the day.
    It's a low-budget morning, shelved in a cabinet of a storm

-flung dawn, and I want nothing bigger than you, nothing
    better or new. Few times, we've cried in this room. Still,

the remnant is a song that patters your lips alone, as if it's a thin,
    haloed path, on which the most nourished years weep

underneath and become the rootlets of a tree. What clatters
    in the ghost that micro-cooks this plate? What meal this mild

and motherly is lesser than a miracle? You and I bike
    in the wind like a word blown out of an ancestral tongue,

flung into a moment as small as this. Sleep again, mom.
    Wake up in my tilt. Shove the departed night into the tilted

cup, while the pillow cushions the world within our breath.
    How many musketries of snores do you clench? What platoon

of praises breaks out of your voice like a squirrel? The wind
    is beggarly. It's whooshing outside. Its voice is a wheel of fire

and fur, finding the peels of our windows, a storm oozing
    out of what spills, filling our bellies with a rostrum of rinds,

suctioning juice out of a pantry we never had. Breakfast
    on the bed, lunch in a rosebud of mire, dinner in a den,

doubting we were ever here. Worry softly, mom. Think less
    of the things I don't know I lack, think more of this moment

as though it were a pulse. Pause, when you can
    only start, and begin with me on this metronome of silence,

this blister of your touch; your stare and your sigh, your loin
    lyre and love singing down like the tenderness of grace.

II

Familial caws
For Laide

Down the small, edible park, a bird falls
like utterance on my tongue, while I watch

you and the baby laugh like two sweet solvents
under the severed sun. Here we are, three ballots

cast into a morning plucked out of the stimulant
that hangs on the equator of longing, three rib

-bons of fire dropped on the circumference
of our thirsts. When this boy becomes a tree,

and you and l, wind-ripped an autumn past,
storm-felled a winter old, what seascape would hum

the souls of the fruits that wobble out of him?
What rootlets would be the parcel sampled

thickly out of the memories of our lungs?
He's the finest gossip out of us, a small cherubic

dialogue that babbles wisely like a cohort
of words and water. And the morning combusts

into noon, and rain subsumes us and buries
us in a capsule of flowers, and we run

down the path that pleads for home, feeling
the cadence of hunger in our tidal bellies,

feeling our son so close, like a souvenir
of warmth easing out of our woven bones.

A kneeling flower

There will be you at dawn,
seated on the quake of a song
-encrypted dark, pointing at our secrets
in the soot of the sky we still call
clouds these days, and arranging our souls
like two moments welded into memory.
There will be silence but it will not
be silent. A tension of fluid will splash
wildly like bird calls. Call it rainfall,
but it's something crisper, like grief,
like rust, like the lament underneath
us, when, each day, we hurl our bodies
into a country that longs to hurl itself
into us. Like each soul, a flag made
of thorns, of ripe stings, juicy prickles,
like the home in your palm, bittersweet
like absence, feverish like longing
borrowed from the wormhole
of a kiss. Still, my bone will scrape
yours, your glance will spade mine,
and we'll walk into a shapely enclosure
of wings and whirl, sculpting a word
that will bleed a world, knowing
every aim at love is a stare at loss,
at sculpting a dropping of breath,
at believing every wrist ajar is as open
as a soul as open as a kneeling flower.

Her far-fetched song

I lie, tonight, on the edges of my mother's yawn,
and hammer my memory and feel the tang of rust

on my soul, as though tar had fallen hard on my heart
like rotten notes. Rain on the roof stutters. Each drop

hesitates as though uncertain of its song, as though
doubtful of its celestial dive, as though its lips

could hurt the already miry ground. Still, I sniff
my mother's glance and fatten like a flood. A cast

of ants sponges the dust and plasters the wind. Mother
pulls me into her story, where I linger in the conflict

of silence and noise. Down there, sounds are open
-mouthed, places are pauses peeling off the scars

we forever share. My body roots itself here,
in this weather whose mirror is pith and blossom.

And down the woods, a bouquet of dust spreads wide
like a cloud of lenticels. Chirrs of rootlets sprint

like honey-suckles of breath. Mother hums
out of the residue in her belly, each route

is a song she rides tenderly into comfort. And brown
clouds cry for long, stars weep into a melody

of memories. I stiffen, refusing every motion,
becoming the dishes of the night, becoming the itch

for her aged songs, unlearning all my sighs,
and sadness, until I'm nothing but my blankest self,

from which she pours and pours her idioms, her bright
phrases which spin in the dark, taking all of me

along, leaving all of me to thrum, and rain, and to moor
and minstrel like the melody of dreams.

Recollections

Memories cry at home. Each
　　　　　　　a bubble bled on the pages we've become.
A folio of the moments we've piled up here, all of which ages like you, like
the tambac
of your tongue, ceding its copper
　　　　　　　-strung sounds, forfeiting its secrets
and lyrics on our spines. Tonight, I erect a burr of warmth

in my mouth and walk
　　　　　　　into the room, where cheap toys stack themselves
as though waiting for some redemption. But they're all alone. They wipe off
the dust
dressed like doubts, teething
　　　　　　　the whistles in my heart, sliding down the ground
of my once slender, childhood affections. And they sniff

flat-hatted wave of ashes,
　　　　　　　which is a song that springs off a tasteless
tongue weaponed with a spade. We accumulated a family here, accumulated
a pair
of disembodied creeks, spiritual
　　　　　　　gardens, fistfuls of contentment, and sang
ourselves into a world never asleep. And today, I sniff

tomorrow in bucketfuls of roaches.
　　　　　　　Riding through the dark, I imagine
what this tuning fork sprung off my eyes tenders mercilessly warm. What
does a decade
here as a boy accumulate in the belly
　　　　　　　of a man? And what droppings of a bird
or berry run up on my soul? There's Kusama's *Accumulation*

on my mind, that armchair
                    that looks like a tableau of newsflash knifing
through one's dream, the paintings escalading like a vision of violins deliv-
ered by the lip
-sticks of the dark, handcrafted
                         objects that could hum and hole a bathtub
of sleep, her phalluses, feminine with strength, like the fabric

of mercy, sewn out of my mother's
                         veins, threads of spots on geysers
that core us out, the furnace on the tongues we coat with tales. And so
everything
salts away in a grille, scuttles
                         scattered like voices on the slit of our time-sewn
mattresses. And I remember all this by forgetting

the rain still rains, the sun still suns,
                         summering on absence until a missile
of winter pushes me into a breeze, so cold like hotness torn, like warmth
wrinkled,
like a conglomerate of prayers
                         buzzing out of my mother's secret hive,
where tonight I taste myself in a herringbone of silence,

in a woven claw of wishes worn,
                         and I become a gathered song, a bee gum
tongued and thronged, becoming a boy again, dressed in your lullaby, low-
ered down
a crib with my cries soaring high
                         like hungry wrens above my head.

Disappearing

A sputter of secrets, a sea emptying into a vase
refilling itself with singing. An arm carrying

a hundred sailors like heartbroken lilies, cast
away from all their lives into a sweet fossil

of waders. But it's a low-priced afternoon,
and the breeze recruits an echo and paints

the face of the world with a weather suddenly
loved. Here we are, two caked cries,

two svelte sighs, going nowhere. Somewhere,
though, this sail will harden into rail. Dusk

will drip into our journeys, and I'll walk
you into an urn corked with a long lineage

of sweet, muscling ash. Rudder me low. Split
this silence into songs. Sing and sigh and wait

for the shot performed like a flower. For I'm
with you like an organ cuddling its own knife.

Like a sore unhewn from sour to soul. From soul
to song, from song to stern and helm and hull.

The water—a teardrop of the sky and clouds—
hardens like a jaw sculpted by scoop of ebbs,

like a page reciting its own body, pretending
to end, pretending to dip into the soil. And then

your hand reaches for me, a scratch piercing
against on my infinitely itchy shoulder, inching

its taste onto its own tongue, like a sting that sticks
two petals into the slither of a wind-ripped song.

Reappearing

My body is a kiss of wounds, an unsharpened fruit
rolling down a cliff of longing. But I'm buoyed

like a vow in your arms, pressed against the love-edge
of your body, and everything seems like it would be

alright. They don't want us woven, or knotted like a tongue,
but dawn today, a wound finds us and bleeds

us into blood-deep coins, tossed from tongue to tongue,
from a petal of grief to a leaflet that pleases

like grace. Give light to the nectar of the trodden,
strip silence off a sepulcher of calm. Your name

on my tongue is graffiti, fitting like fire, thoughtful
like rain. And it is dawn, but the world puts on a molten

curtain, semi-dark, and our souls couldn't decline
both any quicker. In the room, you deflate each bruise

as though each were a route into rain, the one that naps
on a corpse until it sips all the cries of the bereaved.

The one that knows how a ballad strums a bone.
How beauty beats and stutters from the inside.

How solids howl into vapor. So I believe in the prosody
of a kiss, the thawing of a sigh, the hug that leaves

us with no arms. I believe in vowels and the body
of a word, say its spine, for instance, or its mouth,

or its blade-peeled torso suffused in singing oil.
When you sing, your voice encases me in a clench

-sung summer, and I sleep with my eyes waxen
like dusk. And dust on my skin bends

over like recovery. Still, every silence soothes a finger,
every finger finds its fire along the way, like you

and I, two eloping plovers, loving the nest that cries
out with the currencies of deserted belonging, and firing

smoothly with the tender ironing of broken skins.

Renewal

An arm of rainfall hangs
                on our voices tonight, a province shuffles
in our conversation, as I look into the deep pocket of your being, hearing
cities
cry like flags in your belly,
                  while we talk, as lines bulge out like rays
out of the dark. Still, your eyes are shanghaied mutters.

Each blink vowing like a song
                  spilling out of a clench. But I just want
to stare at your body of berries forever and never unsee you again, and never
unhear
you, never unroot you.
                I just want to know you the way an itch knows
its scratch. I just want to unseal your breath

like belonging. And behind us,
                the rain reaches for the ashes that fell
off your departed flask of silence. And as I touch you, veins recoil like shop-
worn
vowels, my mouth becomes
                a walk, becomes a stride awash with grief
in the gooseneck of our memories. Please, take me

on a walk, again. Let's leave
                our bodies behind and roam as free
as a chirp uncased by a bird-flung page, a sigh disrobed by a wildness of paw
and power meshed and unmeshed
                into a gentle peel. And we stand on the night
and the moonlight buoys us like a steam, and screams

of yesteryears spin like murmurs

                        in our ears, and we go, parting
the night like the fire in a fruit, like the splitting in a kiss, like Macke's *Sun
-light Walk*, except this is a moon

                           or a tarmacked sun, except this is a night
or a stuccoed noon, where, feasting on the breezes

that diminish behind you,

                   I come alive in your memory, once again,
like a leaf, and a branch, and a mountain shrinking into the dew with its
belly
unfastening into songs.

Copestones of the belly

Thyme in a navel, the sting smooth like a cut
woven in a kiss, the neckband of night circling

a moonlit rain, naked like a shrouded song
on the sofa of the soul. We walk into the emerald

of home and become two eels sublimed into vapor
and vows. Poultices of mud, pastas of patterned

sands, tinseling the paths with gravels of singing.
Each song is a flame in the fist of rain. Each path

a whirlybird in birdless robes. A rose, tonight,
floats like a robe reeking of petal and blood,

like you and I, two lean rosebuds, uprooted here
into a sweet, smooth devotion of flames,

into a monologue of fire, into a question that keeps
asking itself a question, that keeps ransacking

the night, the wind, the dark flung into the mildest
copestones of the belly.

Growth is a trim treble

At home, grief is twofold,
                              but one casts its shadow
on the console of my silence, a silhouette as shapely as the line
of a song the sun grips and hurls when uncased.
                              Salty ballots of vowels,
each a clenched sigh, each unhinging my body like the blade

that bends on the cork of a tape
                              -red tongue. And when I wrap
the femur of the sadness I'm dealt in fuchsia, your gold eyes crack
the butterflies that leap off the spittle
                              of a flower, and I gift
all my breathing to you, all my secrets in sighs

and signs, the empires of my fears,
                              lipsticks of my doubts,
the circumference of a glance creaking like what crows in the nostril
of a snake. Love, at times, is worship,
                              a bled devotion, a fever
-ish belch deepening in the belly of mercy. Cut me open. Taste the thyme

of my bones, the one squeezed
                              out of the memories a mother
pan fries on her birthday, the one juiced out of the gourd that grills
a city into rain. I bleed vowels.
                              I leak lexicons of scented
clangs. I'm the bell on the nail of a belly, a navel

as a nation, nudging into a phrase
                              as perfumed as the ghost
of a petal suctioned in the tamarind of oil. And today, let's make
a night by cuddling the dark
                              that's sewn into the nectar of noon.
Let's make the room a womb of fallen hair, treeing

our tongues, until each word
                              we hurl shoots out a stem,
a place like the taste of a plover's skin, like the lace that slithers
out of singing on a possum's
                              feet, becoming the cry of creases
on a piebald palm. Becoming a creek. Becoming the water that weeps

on the monologue of sleep.
                              Becoming me when I stretch
like the relic of a mile, like the distance between grief and growing,
between home and a foot
                              outside a bleeding, broken door.

A cuddle births a world

I still spit at my childhood with a vow. I still bleed
the pages of my flesh. I still steam my soul

in oral fluid, so down this grief-soluble road, I fetch
for you in the mercury of seeing, in the magma

of staring, in the innards of a memory in clay
and clouds. I have no home save this bone, lifted

from a thousand thrones that compose my bright,
slender skeleton, but when I kneel in your fire,

I sniff motherhood in empires of herbs. And I sense
a skin breathing, dim like death in a keyhole,

as sleek as the tongue in a tide swallowing its spoken
tunnel. And still, I want no edifice save this body

which promises never to bloom away. And I want
to know why a kiss is a hiss flavored

or savored afresh. So hiss on my lips and let
me wear the relics of a kiss, and let's seethe

like the rust that flags a tongue. All day I wear
the marrow of the morning and move,

slowly into your edible snow, where your weeping
cakes like a wind, where I burn loneliness

in the corners of the room's loneliest cries,
where I fling on top your posture like a glance,

and dance out of the clench on the laments of my legs,
knowing only a body makes a home, only a cuddle

births a moving world.

III

A heart-ripped flame

Exile cries in my belly. A story rides down my veins.
So how can I be free if I'm still bound, if I'm still laced

to a sore fruit, if I'm still trussed to a foot with blood
spilling down its loneliest shores? I'm the flagellum

of dark, the organelle of thirst, as whispery as sleep,
awake as dying when accompanied by a stolen tongue.

Still, I slither out of the silence no one loves to hum.
I slither out of my country's sigh once more,

and, on a mothball of breath-depleting light, I learn
of my body as memory. I learn of my lips as windfalls

on the rear of bleeding. I learn of my thighs as highs,
of my throat as lows. And I learn of you as muscular

absence, as osseous longing, as a place interred in a path
painted void. The night mistakes itself for tar, zincing

all of our throats, as smooth as the shroud hurling
our voices like edible coins tossed low into our stuccoed

sleep. But sleep is tossed too, slow and whole, like a child
left all alone in warm maternal murmurs, learning

what part of growing is mud or mire, what part of healing
is bleeding or love, bathing or blood, learning

what part of a song is as spacious as the thought springing
out of a silence unclenched by its bone, what part

47

of motherhood is just the hood, what part of parenting
is a mother machining her umpteenth universe all alone,

all at home like a miracle tended by its own flame.

All warmth is woven

The scar a smile   the open wounds
of a hand-ripped flower   of rain dripping down
like sandbars from an uncorked vial   This is
home   shrinking every year   as if my siblings
and I are recoiling   are diminishing back
into the silence of a womb   into the belly
of a storied ancestor   But tonight   mother
folds like a fruit   her tree is felled   her twig
is a howl with a pen-punctured gourd   We refill
her tonight   My sister holds her by the peel
by a horde of wireless memories stretching
out like broken limbs   This rubble is sweet
and sour   and I have no tongue to give
save a bone plucked off my sleep   which limps
from rot to root like a tempered flower
Love plays when the music of the world sighs
back into its body   Here we are
a family whose ink pours like fire
whose words open like a throat   whose line
is a lyre weeping into a town   We heal
on fumes   and squeeze out of a feast
and let the night knot like moon-sliced
songs on our bodies   This distance so near
this history so torn and sewn like a finger
-knitted warmth

Sighs are electric

A song falls on the neck of the night, where, these days,
it's been lightning for light, roar for rain, noise broken

out of the oven of the country's skin. Thunderer of the Nile,
how much charge and charm, hushed in the hovel

of your fields, still floats? How much of the 28th century
still belches in you like a sunblind? In the *De Magnete*,

Gilbert wrote *electricus* on our hardbacked tongues.
Like amber. Something about that color, whose frame

is a fossil sweetened by the rain. And something
about the resin itself, reeking of secrets and songs,

widening a leaning for the light, the trimming of a triumph
this tiled and snowclad. All my life I'd lacked a resin

this colorful, a risk this worthy. I'd left the fossils
of my belly to deepen into a pulseless dark. Tonight,

you hold my hand and the chapel of the dark comes apart
like a finger. And we're in the house, electrified

by mutterings painted before the fire roared, before the flood
fueled a decade off our departure. And here you are,

a leaf-backed ghost, mild as a palm tree, clenching
your hands like a sprig, singing a fume wrapped in a woven

fist. Guericke sent mundane virtues to the staircase
of our bones. It's so routine it's rare, that, in a night

as slender as a hum escaping from a burrow, we burrow
through the jackets of our loneliness, in the cold

as though not, struck by the lightnings of near
and nocturnal eyes, and then a wire of doubt strung

in our mouths fries us into a hiccup of faith, into a root
with a book-bound tongue, and a moment felled by a taste

unstructured like longing leaking out of songs.

A bike and a far-flung song

Childhood stutters out of me, while I stand near my sun
-ripped home. And down the woods, spokes speak

through my breath and spill memories out of my vein
-barred stutter. A word rims a tongue and offloads

its beaver fur on the body. And a scene becomes a being
becomes a kingfish of ironclad feelings. And today, I gear

-shift down the seatpost of the lawn and lie in the morning's
brow, while chainrings teethe, and handlebars hive

the broken clapboards of my wind-strummed veins.
No memory travels faster than a bone. Or blood.

And all day I cog and lever on the lawn and last
like what sprinkles out of a bird-knotted sea. And waiting

for you, mom, the building shrinks by tick-tocking
thickly like the clock hand in the brain. And day after day

tastes like darkness fattening on dawn. But you're aging
like the land and my skin burns on the tar

of what the past thins and tickles on my tongue.
How many wars plumb and ply through a tale?

How many buried bones sing like a rosebud of rooms
in this juiceless ground? Dear iris of light, dear pupil

of purple paths, widen this noon, nudge me nearer
to the nations unsaid in my mother's songs. Nudge me

nearer to what slithers like forgiveness in the wallet
of my silence. There's a path unplowed in my child

-hood. Hurl me there. Bike me through winds
with wishes that walk into the line that severs a bond.

Into the fist that fissures a night- from its -mare. Into a song
saddled with choirs that simmer, and ballads that bleed

and boil, and places that print their oceans on vellums
and voice, and let me be free like the mint on a taste

bud, like the fingers escaping a squirting smoke,
or a spurting fume. Let me be me in my mother's word

-less miracle, the melody of misses and makes, the harmony
of a home built strong on the spare and bare hands

of a million hums.

Beats in a gourd

The sun is a skin tinseled by its ripeness, as bright lights
shiver the taste that unlaces a line. I long to swim into the knife

of your absence and pile a thousand tides of scars, but the water
is wave-worn, wordless and worldly. Mollusks succuss

my tongue, blow a page of eddies into the elms of my eel
-shaved eyes. Love, today, is a broken cup. It cries its content

into a fountain of blades. The stream bulges like a bruise.
You are not here, and the base of the land is a suburb

of slender ghosts. What type of onion out-bulges a balloon?
What type of baobab thrums a ventricle of blood-laden

ballads? The heart, I guess. There's music climbing its stairs
into a tissue of sour, bittersweet tastes. Emotion is flavory.

Hurt kneels in its own hut, easing into a breeze-blown easel
of love. And I come here to remember the weeks that left

before arriving, the months that slapped themselves
against a tsunami of rot welded into silence. And we're

all in a lover's memory, at times. And most times, in ours.
But right now, I'm stiffened like a wind wanted

by nobody's mind or mouth. I'm wanted by nobody's past,
so I splash the phrases of the water into my breath and breast

-stroke through the water's blue-wild worship of rays.
There's a haven in hushing oneself into a moment made

by a mugful of music and mystery. There's a tunnel in the light
flung out of an oyster's eyes. I turtle and crab. I clam

and squid. I shellfish my body and my bones creep
out of the unbound book I've become. My paperback skin

is drenched and will not be dried again. My tongue
is the only surviving page. Strum me. Lash my luminance

of tails. Make a salted vowel out of the shore hammered
like berries onto my palms. When you come (if you come),

come like a sown idiom, like a sewn touch. Come like a wader
with the wages of warmth, and will my volume into a brace

-let of blood, into a waistband of sweet, sour, ebb
-accompanying love.

Fire in a petal

The light is a peel and a prairie alloyed, a belly of rays
and ruin, laughter and liquid, a noon with a raiment

of thorns. I'm an escaping fabric of body and air, searching
for a land that would open my fleshly borders. Tonight,

the breath you suctioned off my lungs whistles here.
It's found me near and naked, and I want no clothes

to taste my body save a dream, and I'd wait for a night
bold enough, a night void of nightmares, a night wooden

and burry, prickly like a proverb, on which I'll wade
into a country of snores and settle like a sniveling note,

and note, once again, the sweetly spaciousness of sleep,
the provinces that pile like paintings on its carpet

and tongue. I'll denaturalize my bongo drums of doubts,
and walk out of my wake asleep, awake like hush

in silence, like splash in rain, like tide in water.
I'll awaken like a clatter of sleeping acorns.

And freedom would leap into my snore and snarl
me until I'm unshackled, and your growl would grill

me the way a vocal grills a beat, the way a million songs
sleep on a bone, and awaken a vinegar of memories.

And rain would fall into my sleep and crack a vowel,
my new land and tongue, my new hoarseness of flowers,

my new petal of peace and place, of fire and feelings
and fuel.

Leaping bullets

The wind is rough like a lean afternoon—a sour compost
falling off the throat of a forest flamed beneath our sleep.

And I long for the solvent of your soul, the silhouette
of your sighs, the cushion of your body's icicles, to tail

my bleeding bracelets into the tender noon. The house,
for instance, is chopped like a tide. It spills onto the rug,

and my body breaks like a chirp weeping for its young
beneath a tooth-sharp mound. Still, we're in a ghost's torn

pocket, it seems, and I rest on the knife-hem of your breath,
leaking like an aubade knuckling out of my longing.

At home, the wall is heavy with a woodpile of sighs.
Silence erupts like a scream returning from a trip

it cannot remember. And your loss tastes like herbs
in my stomach. Your breath sings like the stammering

falsetto of my footfalls. And I hold you longer than I've
lived, studying the soot of rife blood in your eyes,

holding the edges of the afternoon like a scar, loving
you with the grief that grows, with the sorrow that soars

like leaping bullets inside my belly.

The soul's an apron

Darkness is light napping on the sepulcher
of its flowers, at rest like the evening in a mother's

eyes, seasoned like a soul, sun-sliced like the voice
that lends itself to fire. But flame is sweet

and sour. There's something about the fossils leaping
off a hug-ripped feeling, as savory as the tongue

on the tree bark of a brain, as soft as a pile of memories
burning on the wrapper of the mouth. That circle

in a body, orbiting into pale pulses. And when I found
you, I became the stutter of your weeping, the asterisk

burning in your silence. And if we leak out of our bodies
today and spill into forever, how lean and colorful

would be the apron of our souls? How braided
would be that barrel that sings us into murmur?

Spittle on the soul is a vow. Rust on a tongue
is promise. There's no word without a bone, or a tone

slung like footnotes into the oyster of our silence.
We're all bleeding slangs, hurled from a distant

petal, from a far-flung ballad of blood, so today,
unhorse beside me, as low as this slow, bordered,

dismounted song, and fling us into fire, into freedom,
into the habit of a howl as tessellated as love.

Stutter of separation

A cry asleep in our bellies,
                        a thigh of sunshine cast against our necks,
while you and I, raspberries of rumors, rail into the city to leap into a differ-
ent song.
There was a route, now there's
                        a roar, your body issuing out of the morning
like a sigh out of a bruise, like a tale out of the sea,

which today, you pull along
                        like the music weeping in a flood,
like the dark that shadowed each dawn split into the rain that nurses the
corsage
of our kiss. Sometimes
                        going away is the only pathless note that sings
us back. And a closed route is sometimes an open vowel,

or vow, and you and I, two
                        flooded roads, seek just one route,
en route this prosody of dreams, where, as the morning howls like a clock
buttoned with three flicking
                        tongues aflame, I become an untarred
underlip of grief, as empty like a bottomless touch,

as lean as mercy muttering
                        in a souffle-like mud, and still, right there,
the train trails on, while we stare at the tarp of our own disappearance, at
the bell
-bottom seaquake undressed
                        like dissatisfaction, hanging in our bellies
like a doubt, and then I wither into weeping, knowing

how stories like this decompose
                                  on a body, knowing how solitude
sours and scourges a moment, knowing how this morning will become the wreck
that swallows a night, the song
                                  that plucks its own skin, ravaging on,
such that, alighting once more, I'll hold you in one

spot forever, never letting go,
                                  until this distance tapers off a chandlery
of tongues, tapers off the woodbine that would bind and bring us back home
like a whirlpool of severed winds.

All the memories that froze

The sigh of the wind is bottomless. Birds cry in its belly,
curved like the brier of a bone. Silvervines of memories

saddle on it, like a wrap of lilies, like the absence that trails
me when I shrink into the cheekbones of the night.

Down here, the towpath is an unsung lung, locked
with falsettos of air oozing out of the woods. Orbits

of bird routes stretch like language resisting imminent
extinction. Like Rodin's *Walking Man*, for instance:

its stance, its legs, which Sandburg says *hold a torso
away from the earth*. But you bring mine back to earth,

which flames on the caesura of a world
creeping out of your palms. Your hair is the bristles

tonight. It tastes like fire. Semi-sweet, but spicy.
And if I open my skin, what shade of honey would leak

out of me? What pose would a blood this cold sculpt
out of a silence this close? I taste my solitude and lie

on its bloodied veins. I raven the panpipes of the route
and sniff a packet of leaflets leaping into worship.

Without arms I grab your ghostly branchlets and a cry
of longing branches out of me. And my frame,

though headless, creeps ahead, and arrowworms
of questions wire themselves around my tongue,

and your tongue, a mugful of sagittas, and my mouth
too, a cupful of chorus, and if I weren't born,

I would have been sculpted by a brain as mirthful
as you. I would have been here still, all away

from your tongue-sewn gown, cawing like a collision
of rosebuds, singing like a petal of plea.

IV

A tongue is a route

I know you're still bruised from a look wrung
out of oil coursing a decade ago. I know

you're still conversing with the nightmare buried
in a fur that whispers like a bottle in your bone.

Tonight, you sit next to me and a garden dots
our bodies like the embryo of spittle, and I hear

your silence loud, as though a cry could tide,
even for a while, on bright leaves squeezing

out of what a soul strums in a hundred dactyls
that dance within your mouth, and, as the world

flips open the broken pages of dusk, you cry,
and I cry too, with the sweet leaflets of your lungs,

having lost all of mine to longing, yet, what silence
splits like the body of a kiss? What vowel plants

a song on what a mouth fins and fires? I know
what I sniff when your hair perches on my skin

like a mood with a coil clicking like a tongue.
Your hair, those tamarinds of wires, gnarls

like the climate of a cushioned vein. And we go
on unlearning our wounds, undoing our bruises

which creak like the towel of a touch, like the sound
that chases a mood into the island of what falls,

into the valley of what dances off the sour tarmac
of a flag of tongues.

A swaddling breath

All of longing is a song scraped off the sidewalls
of our bones. And where I sit, down the yawn

of this slaughterous sun, the wind is a small, jellied
bladder. Landscapes hiss with sun-clenched miracles.

The moment is tucked with three tongues tickling
its spine, and they sigh and sing and whistle

out of the window of a loss. Three. Scheele who found
it. Priestley who wrote it. Lavoisier who coined it.

The way they mailed oxygen into the cradle
of our historical lungs. Three, mom. You, dad and I.

'Cause everything, even the songs papering
our oblique souls, even lullabies gnawing our loins,

having discovered us, long to be discovered again.
Daylight grips the lawn and trisects the dark.

Birds crosscut like petals furrowing on an aged
tongue. And near the garden which often enwraps

us, I'm tomahawked by thoughts whittling down
like home. But every soul is a foot fired from a belly

hollowed out of a family. And every eye is an urn
in which absence burns itself on the jaw of singing.

Why do I think I could outrun the wind waiting
on the bedside of my blood? Why do I think a lineage

isn't a knife: scarred as the body it pokes? Why
aren't my lips as mean and musical as a beak picking

up a flower? The rivers on the rump of the moat
deepen and dry up like the rivers within us.

When I watch them these days, I become a lean,
skeletal watercourse, thirsty like the estuary that hangs

on our whiskered breath. And by noon, I go
where silence goes, where a scream has always known;

here, far away from every motherly mud,
from every maternal manure, from every song sifting

selflessly like breathing, like aging, like returning
to the breath that first returned me to you as a long, lean

swaddled bouquet of warmth.

A monologue on fire

We float like flanks on the stadia of the water,
knowing, in you, I hold on to the song I long

to rain into. But all year, we feuded, and ended
each word like a bridge, and blunted every glance

plumed out of our lives. But here you are again,
water spading water, finning with my body

into a flush of sacred plums. But who knows
the stove-blue fist of an orphaned flame

and where it rusts in a body? Who knows
how the apron of a flower becomes an idiom

flung off a palm? And who knows how the tail
of a memory sneezes into the feathers that rake

the mind, or what shore our dreams shovel
in our sleep, which dactyl is which, a finger

or a foot, who touches the pulse that's spat
out of a vase? Here, love. Sit on the lining

of a million tides spitting into us like fire.
Like flood. Like flourish. And sit on the sepulcher

of rain, bleed me with a love this corporeal,
this volatile, this slaughterous like a small,

bristling tongue. All day I fatten on eddies
and all the griefs crying like spiracles in my belly

ebb. The seasons on my tongue spill on the door
-mat of our hands. We taste gills, touch

peduncles, sniff spiny-rayed fins. We're bladders
bulging out of waves. We're antennas gardened

by oars. And you wanted the mood that sugars
a river into books, and here it is, a sleeve of water,

lumbered down our veins like the spittle of hunger.
And dusk chases us and we hide our mouths

in the murmurs off the tunnel of ourselves. That feverish
light tucked at the tail end, that song wagging away

like a soft, smooth, barefoot clench of memories.

Circadian citizen

What is that light breaking out like flowers
in our silence? What is that song showering

down our bones when we stare at our bodies
like sun-sliced stones, like two notes dipped

in the oil dripping off a matchbox? I'm aflame
in your mouth awash. Spill me if only I'd whisper,

if only I'd seep out of you like a mutter easing
out of a vein, if only a nerve would tuck

me back to this century of silence, in which,
in a dawn this deep like a rootbound clench,

no word cracks, no phrase fissures a vial of fear,
no place encases us like a bitten pause.

The night, though, will come, if, seated
on this umbilical dawn, darkness peels

off a footfall in the years lined like light-columns
between our souls. The morning falls

on our tongues and rain cracks the crevices
of our thirst. I sit next to you like a sentence

hammered against the wall, and we talk,
because nothing but words linger

still in the flour of the life we've thrummed
here, and as I hold your wattage of hair

-bristles, I freeze into a fingered lily, tempered
by a rose, like a dose of salt written

sweetly on your glance, penned softly
like a song banded with inflection

on our tiny beaming lungs.

A decade on my wings

You and I are bodies compressed into flowers.
Tonight, the year doesn't start until a kittened

door fruits. Until our blood leaps into the bosom
of a spaded sky. Until what I see are whiskers

of open spaces falling off your mouth. Yet,
this is not why I wanted you ajar at the muzzle

of my stare. This is not why I wanted you bent
over my breath like a buried flank. There comes

a time when no melody of time blossoms
but a body of emptiness, making the leaflets

locked in my belly an empire of longing.
Light peels off my ribs, and I taste what dances

off the cuticle of a dream, what tiptoes like coins
within silence. And still, thirst is the only extant

koine bruised and bloodied like freedom
on my tongue. Hunger is a limb plumped

out in the plums that soothe my belly.
And does freedom ever exist without a broken

creek begging to sing? Does a chain fondle
when it ages and gnarls? This country doesn't

want us clothed in plain-woven songs,
so somewhere on the tusk of the night, I hide us,

learning what udder of darkness to trust,
what mammary memory to mist over our silence,

what open choruses creep out of a fist
that will not ripen, and even now, what hollowed

love unroots the shackles soaring with a decade
on their wings.

Foretaste

If you sail on the suburbs of my blood you'll soar
on the mouth of a sentence. Rail here. Pedal softly

like a song. Sniff a phrase on the petals of my arms.
Let me take you by the hand and grip you

with my sweetest cry. The sprout whose throat leaks
of laughter. The bloom whose bombs tick and tame

your tongue, whose frame sniffs a million scars
off your hoisted soul. That swelling so telling of blood

and bone. That beginning with a beautiful bruise.
There's a baby in your mind tonight, swaddled

in the warmest crib-cry you've ever heard. That, too,
is *bud*. Brain. Blood. That, too, is your face shrunk

to its fittest, all your flaws finished to *dear, darling*
and dazzle. How many dreams bloom in us

by dying inside the dig of their own blood,
yet we've been made to think we're not seeds

or trees or trunks. But we are. Like this cedar elm,
chorusing green and gravy, we bend and unbend,

we swing and sling our fortunes into the sweetest
peppers of the soil, and we grow, and leaving

this sentence, we know, one day, even the poorest
soils, the penniless spots, will flower. Birds will shower

their droppings on our birdless parts, and wounds
will heal like rootlets, and every soil will be a soul

again, sailing with an army of sown and recovering
anklets of songs.

Chasing silence

I roll into the night like a die with a dangling
flame. I walk on a tumult of glances and grass,

watching a shoal of buildings bow into the oven
of voluminous lights, watching nocturnal idylls

of frogs flog through the belching muds. A nation
begins with a nudge, and mine hasn't begun,

save for nightly flowers souring like language
dented by a quake of prickly-edged leaves. Save

for salts splashed on the eyes of a thousand souls
bent over their sacred murmurs like ghosts. Save

for you, beginning again, in my bone like a far
-flung ballad, like a moon-slung sigh, like the sneeze

that encases its reflex and unwraps it in the knee
-jerk of a surprise. My legs step a different dark

in a different route towards the river route.
What does a pregnant dark kitten or pup?

What second night would slither out of its mouth?
Tonight, I want to kneel in your own night,

which an hour ago, flipped into daylight, the way
you've always been ahead, even now, your hours

a branchlet of sun-beaming rings. Mine the dark
of the dark that tautens, of rods raining and running,

of each wood a womb of wombat-lit candles,
swooping into their swollen pockets. Does a marbled

frown sing? Do souls text other souls the news
of their own shrinking? Maybe if I'm tossed

or flipped my other side would splatter on your scar
-decked palm, but you're not here, so I walk the weeping

wind towards the fence line. I out-flicker the sleepy
-eyed moon, and my body hums, exhaling the many chords

inhaled off your candle-echoed name, the countless
routes that scratch the lean shaddocks of your fluted,

fitted breath.

The diaphragm of home

Back home it ached to sniff like oceans do:
tides enlarging their diaphragms, tunneling

through a flock of lungs like devotion. Back home
secrets seeped out of a bone, platelets

with their own tales, their own books, wagging
like pages from a baby's mouth down

to the tail she exuded like a fruit. At home,
I'm taught by a cohort of loneliness. Each

a colubrid of questions, slithering down
like galaxies gagging me in my sleep.

In a country be a country of silence. Know
which to store and which to sell, which to buy

and which to borrow. I borrow your sounds,
a reptile of bodiless rhymes, seated at my mother's

stone-broke garden, feeling the sun like a stolen
sequel of daylight. Maybe dusk's not

all it's cracked up to be. Maybe darkness
is just my dream, my wish in a factory

of historical warmth. But I'm loved today
by this anthill that unwraps a lean gift shot

out of my mother's childhood, where she thinks
the world as mild as a child, where she thinks

the world was kinder like a wind, where she thinks
the world loved her climate and pouched

her right the way a wombat pouches her young.
Where she longs someday to hurl me to,

as if to rewind me, sometimes wishing
she'd rehearsed me earlier before performing

me in her womb. Still, every home out there looks
like mine, manured by a woman, a mother

ministering her sighs, her pages of assuasive
sounds, her moments of mystery, her moments

of awe.

A tempered song

The plover is a dream in bed with a manuscript
of scars. Woods creep out like footfalls

off a journey in oldie and bleats. The moment
is musical like a small, chapleted dream.

But truly, it's a circus. The *Cirque Calder*.
A unicyclist of flowers swarms my body

as though I were a peel plucked out of a petal.
And what quivers in me is what shivers

the loincloth of the landscape. Hoopers
with wooden hoops, hollowed out like longing

out of their duffels of bones. It is a musical
war, sounds in gourds and girdles, frozen

like forever, unfreezing into an exit-kittened
wind. I have buried a handful of dear ones,

but this afternoon I long to sculpt a life,
or breath, or a fist of voices. The land clangs

and starts in trapeze and seethes like aprons
with a million fobs of teething shocks.

Why jugglers, if not to show how dreams
are tossed out of the dark into the bowels

of the future. A kiss is like hiss. Songful.
And sorrowful, at times. Like the dotted bone

of a berry, split into a creek of fulminant
clocks, thrown into the belly of a metal-cutting

calm. And still, I linger like a stare in the landscape.
My life murmurs like a cracked calabash

of choruses, like a gourd of choirs, like a moment
made swollen by a stack of tempered songs.

Walking

The door opens to a fire-warm dawn, a spot aflame
with birds. Outside, the wind is a word spilled

out of a plover's mouth, and my body is a book
shelved in a grass sprouting out of a tongue

that cracks like absence. Within solitude a song
is scorching, a voice is a scar flung out of a rusted

roof that leaks. Still, I walk into a morning singing
like a gong of currants. My village is a vehicle.

My home a rim. There are sands scratching my mourn
-ful soles and sending signals to the part

of my brain that pens your distance as doubt.
And I wait at the crying creek whose waves shrink

like a clime clenched in a baby's fist. I sense
its rise and fall in my belly the way fear bleeds

and belches, the way my mother's glance
once jarred me, hurling me to the ground

of my chores. All roads, I guess, reek
of memories, and the route in my palm spreads

into the brown barren woods behind me.
At home I'm a bone shrouded in wishes unpacked

from my childhood ears. I'm uncrated like a glass
in my mother's dream-hurled stare. A parent's

longing is lean and long, stretching out, reaching
you anywhere. And dawn today, I die like breath

in the water, diving, washing the moment in a scratch
of widowed splashes. And this is the rain

I want drenching my tongue. This is the drizzle
I want in the unpierced pocket of my shoe-size lungs.

Acknowledgments

At the time of writing the poems for this collection, "Scars of utterance" placed Second in the 2020 *Into The Void Magazine* Poetry Prize. I'm thankful to the editors and judge for giving this poem a place.

Thank you to my good friend, the poet Adeeko Ibukun, for the chats, the critiques, and the friendship. Thank you, 'Gbenga Adeoba, and to everyone whose poetry and prose I've loved, read, enjoyed, and learned from.

I'm thinking of the professionalism and dedication shown by the New Rivers Press team, beginning with Nayt Rundquist, Kevin Carollo, and everyone who edited and offered feedback to bring this collection to life, and I'm saying thank you. I appreciate all the efforts.

Thank to you to lovely wife, Laide, and my son who already loves reading, Michael. Thanks for the love and understanding.

Above all, thanks to God, for the love and the grace, for the breath and the songs that found me.

About the Author

Samuel Ugbechie has works published or forthcoming in *Ruminate Magazine*, *Slippery Elm*, *Palette Poetry*, *Nottingham Review*, and elsewhere. He's the winner of the 2020 Aurora Poetry Winter Contest and the 2016 Frederick Holland Poetry Collection. His works have been recognized in awards like the Fiddlehead Ralph Gustafson Poetry Prize, Janet B. McCabe Poetry Prize, Vice-Chancellor's International Poetry Prize, Into the Void Poetry Prize, and others. He tweets @sugbechie.

About New Rivers Press

New Rivers Press emerged from a drafty Massachusetts barn in winter 1968. Intent on publishing work by new and emerging poets, founder C.W. "Bill" Truesdale labored for weeks over an old Chandler & Price letterpress to publish three hundred fifty copies of Margaret Randall's collection *So Many Rooms Has a House but One Roof.* About four hundred titles later, New Rivers is now a nonprofit learning press, based since 2001 at Minnesota State University Moorhead. Charles Baxter, one of the first authors with New Rivers, calls the press "the hidden backbone of the American literary tradition."

As a learning press, New Rivers guides student editors, designers, writers, and filmmakers through the various processes involved in selecting, editing, designing, publishing, and distributing literary books. in working, learning, and interning with New Rivers Press, students gain integral real-world knowledge that they bring with them into the publishing workforce at positions with publishers across the country, or to begin their own small presses and literary magazines.

Please visit our website: newriverspress.com for more information.